JAZZ ICONS

WOOD ENGRAVINGS, WOOD CUTS AND PAINTINGS

BY JAMES GILBERT TODD, JR

*Ben — Thought about you
several times at this opening.
Comrade-in-arms ih guess!
Hope this finds you well.*

Jim

Cover: **Dixieland Musician**
watercolor
1964
by James Gilbert Todd, Jr

For

Seamus, Riel, Baird and Families

ACKNOWLEDGEMENTS

Ken Price, Director, UM Printing and Graphic Services
Rick Newby, Poet and Art Historian, Helena, MT
Barbara Koostra, Director, Montana Museum of Art & Culture
Brandon Reintjes, Curator, Montana Museum of Art & Culture
Jim Meinert and the staff of The History Museum, Great Falls, Montana
Yvonne Seng, Curator of Art, Holter Museum of Art
Holter Museum Members and generous supporters of jazz and the arts.

Published on the occasion of the exhibition James Todd: Jazz Icons
Holter Museum of Art, September 7 – December 31, 2012

Design/Layout by UM Printing & Graphic Services and Mezcal and Gusano, Inc., Missoula, MT

JAMES TODD IS PROFESSOR EMERITUS OF ART AND HUMANITIES AT THE
UNIVERSITY OF MONTANA. HE IS A MEMBER OF THE ASSOCIATION JEAN CHIEZE
IN FRANCE, THE WOOD ENGRAVERS NETWORK IN THE UNITED STATES,
THE SOCIETY OF WOOD ENGRAVERS IN ENGLAND AND IS A
SENIOR FELLOW IN THE UK ROYAL SOCIETY OF PAINTER-PRINTMAKERS.
HE HAS EXHIBITED HIS WORK INTERNATIONALLY.

12 East Lawrence, Helena, MT 59601
www.holtermuseum.org

Published by The Holter Museum of Art
© 2012 The Holter Museum of Art

Printed in the United States

JAMES TODD: JAZZ ICONS
HOLTER MUSEUM OF ART
SEPTEMBER 7 – DECEMBER 31, 2012

INTRODUCTION

The Holter Museum of Art is honored to host *James Todd: Jazz Icons* as part of our 25th anniversary celebration. In conjunction with *Jazz Icons*, the Holter is revisiting the Poindexter Collection with which we opened our doors, an iconic group of modernist and abstract expressionist paintings that has left an indelible legacy on Montana's culture and artists. Jazz, with its white pauses (and parenthetical phrasing), improvisation and fleeting suggestions is a natural accompaniment to abstract expressionism and is integral to the work of such artists in the collection as Jackson Pollock, Franz Kline, Sonia Gechtoff and Gene Davis. Likewise, the work of James Todd, a Montana iconoclast, is a natural accompaniment to "the Poindexter", as the Montana Historical Society's collection is affectionately known.

Ornette Coleman said about jazz that "It's the hidden things, the subconscious that lies in the body and lets you know: you feel this, you play this." Jim Todd's prints (and words) capture the "hidden things" of an era and art form. Using simple tools to work the grain of wood, he teases a portrait from between white pauses and dark spaces. In his larger acrylic portraits, jazz musicians and vocalists seem to step out of the shadowed background from which Jim has chosen to release them. Although often solitary and contemplative, as he remarks in the following essay "they are alone masters of their own expressive lives, and there is nothing quite like it."

Even before *Jazz Icons* took up residence on the Holter's gallery walls, the deft hand of Jim Todd began to reveal the hidden. When we received the first prints of jazz women, we gently laid them out on a large library table to breathe. Artist and printmaker Phoebe Toland stepped in between teaching summer classes of young, next-generation artists and joined the silent appreciation, not an unusual response to Jim Todd's mastery. Her first words were a surprise, however: not a comment on technique or form, but a request for her young class who were attempting to sketch their self-portraits to view them. "I want them to see how art can take you inside a person," she said.

In the following essay, "Montana Improvisations: Jim Todd's Jazz Wood Engravings", author and art historian Rick Newby asks: "What is it about Jim Todd's jazz engravings that renders them so captivating?" We have known Jim as philosopher, social commentator, professor and department chair, painter and distinguished engraver. Here, in *Jazz Icons*, we discover him as jazz musician.

The Holter owes a debt of gratitude to the Montana Museum of Art & Culture, without whose assistance *Jazz Icons* would not have been possible. Barbara Koostra, director, and Brandon Reintjes, curator, patiently shared their knowledge, enthusiasm and support for this celebration of James Todd. Our sincere appreciation goes to Jim Meinert and the staff of the Great Falls History Museum for the loan of "Ozark Club", the centerpiece of the exhibition. The Museum would also like to thank members of the Holter community and a peculiar breed of supporter, "jazz enthusiasts", who have made this catalogue, the exhibition, and the supporting public and educational programming a huge success. Lastly, from my heart to Lia Todd, *Danke*.

Yvonne Seng
Curator of Art.

Montana Improvisations: Jim Todd's Jazz Wood Engravings

Painter and printmaker Jim Todd is a true Montana original. While many of his peers paint iconic Montana landscapes, indulge in nostalgic celebrations of pioneer culture, or partake in abstract expressions (that often relate to our vast landscape), Todd participates in a different tradition, one that is resolutely urban (a cosmopolitan urbanism rooted in the Montana experience) and politically engaged. This self-created tradition includes such fierce forbears as early twentieth-century German satirists (Georg Grosz, John Heartfield), Mexican muralists (Diego Rivera, José Orozco), and a wide-ranging roster of other socially committed artists (Käthe Kollwitz, Hannah Höch, Ben Shahn).

Some of Todd's most powerful works reflect what critic Ralph Shikes calls the "indignant eye" – think of Todd's chilling portrait of Chile's General Pinochet and his generals, "Guardians of the Southern Hemisphere", or his nightmarish pair of hand-painted woodcuts, "Las Vegas by Night/Tijuana by Day" – but it can be argued that his most personal work resides in his series of portraits, primarily wood engravings, of jazz artists – a series that stretches from the mid 1960s to the present.

In the grand mythos of the American West, the words "Montana" and "jazz" are seldom linked. And yet this music – which arose in New Orleans out of the collision between African and European musical forms – did find its way to Montana early in the twentieth century, and it continued to flourish well into mid century, especially in urban centers like Great Falls, Butte, and Helena. Of course today a small but vital jazz scene can be found in many Montana cities and towns.

Jim Todd, as he notes in his essay in this catalog, encountered jazz as a young man in Great Falls, where he was enraptured by this wonderfully improvisatory music in local joints like the legendary Ozark Club and through recordings. As recent research on the Ozark Club (visit the Ozark Club exhibit at The History Museum in Great Falls) and black culture more generally (note the Montana Historical Society's recent project, "Uncovering Black History in Montana" shows, African American contributions to Montana's rich cultural mix have been significant and lasting.

During his distinguished career, Jim Todd has made the conjunction of social history and the visual arts a primary focus for both his art-making and his teaching (he taught humanities and art for thirty years at The University of Montana, including a decade as chair of the Department of Art). Jazz, that hybridized, purely American music, became Todd's perfect subject, given his passion for social justice and his lifelong love for the music itself. Jazz has been called the "sound of surprise," embodying a radical freedom, and the history of jazz is inextricably linked with the black struggle in America for equal rights and basic human dignity.

As historian Joachim Berendt writes, "Almost all great jazz musicians have felt the connection between their playing styles and the times in which they live." Both black and white, the jazz players Todd has chosen as his subjects, several of whom came to public attention in the late 1950s and early 1960s, are particularly linked to the Civil Rights movement and to the fight for recognition of jazz as a universal music.

Think of bassist and composer Charles Mingus' "Fables of Faubus" (1959), an enraged protest against the Arkansas governor who called out the National Guard to prevent integration in Little Rock's schools, and his "Meditations on Integration" (1964). Think, too, of bass clarinetist and flutist Eric Dolphy, who became a cause célèbre among his fellow musicians because he died alone and uncared-for in a German jail, a veritable exile from the country he loved because he could not find sufficient work stateside. As saxophonist Archie Shepp wrote of Dolphy, "He died in the tradition of the black artist – i.e., relatively unknown, certainly having been forced all too often to accept work far below his enormous capabilities." Pianist Thelonious Monk, like Dolphy, Mingus, and Charlie Parker (another Todd subject), was a singular innovator, bringing to the jazz tradition a new harmonic freedom coupled with horn-like phrasing, "anchored," as Berendt writes, "in a strong blues feeling and saturated with a mocking, burlesque sense of humor" (qualities not unlike those in Todd's more satiric works; see, for example, the woodcut, "Hitler in Combat", or the acrylic painting, "Aryan Spook".

Another area of social concern for Todd is the role of women in jazz. His portraits of jazz women celebrate the role women have played as preeminent vocalists in the form. Singers like Bessie Smith, Ella Fitzgerald, Billie Holiday, and Anita O'Day have literally been the voice of jazz since the beginning. But it is only slowly that, within this male-dominated music, women have begun to perform in other roles; Todd's portraits of pianists Marian McPartland and Jutta Hipp acknowledge some of the first women to break the gender barrier.

Two other Todd portraits record the enormous change in women's status within jazz in the last forty years. The Japanese-American pianist Toshiko Akiyoshi has broken all the barriers to become the leader of her own big band and a major jazz composer. Perhaps even more impressive, Carla Bley has been a force in jazz since the early 1960s. A founder in 1965 of the Jazz Composers Orchestra, a big band intended to further avant-garde composition and performance, Bley has since the mid 1970s led her own big band and generated some of the most distinctive (and humor-filled) compositions in modern jazz, reminiscent of the work of Kurt Weill. Bley pioneered the notion of independent artist-owned record labels, with her WATT Records, and she founded the late and lamented New Music Distribution Services, which made creative improvised music available to a wider audience, helping to further recognition that jazz is one of the world's great classical musics.

There is no question about Jim Todd's command of the art (and craft) of wood engraving. In the catalog to his 2002 retrospective at the Missoula Art Museum, the renowned British wood engraver Simon Brett wrote that, not only is Todd a master of the medium, but a genuine innovator, breaking the "stereotypes of size and content with which wood engraving is too often associated." By working larger than the norm, Todd increases the impact of his prints, and upon joining the Society of Wood Engravers, he dazzled the British members with the size and "modernity" of prints like his "Mulligan and Monk" (which measures 14 x 11 inches and graced the poster for the Society of Wood Engravers' 1995 75th anniversary exhibition at Oxford's Ashmolean Museum).

What is it about Jim Todd's jazz engravings that renders them so captivating, more so even than his portrait series honoring printmakers (Rembrandt, Jacques Callot, Picasso, Hannah Höch, José Posada) or world changers (Galileo, Charles Darwin, Gandhi)? There is something profoundly grave and dense about these images of jazzmen and women, a bodying forth of lives devoted to exuberant and soulful creativity in the face of very real obstacles: of racism, sexism, and plain old philistinism. This sense of lived experience, hard earned and always passionate, may well come from Jim Todd's early love of jazz, his personal engagement as a young jazz drummer, his sense of a vast world opening up on the fleet notes of Louis Armstrong's trumpet (whom he might have heard at the Great Falls Civic Center, ca. 1950).

No matter the origin of the power of these astonishing portraits, we are fortunate to see them all together, in a single exhibition, to be haunted and moved by their uncompromising dignity, their quiet sorrow, their joy.

– Rick Newby

Jim Todd's prints and drawings, including his portrait of saxophonist Charlie Parker (1973), illustrate Rick Newby's first book of poems, *A Radiant Map of the World* (1981).

HIGH SCHOOL PENCIL DRAWINGS
1954-1958

Terry Gibbs - Vibes

Ray Brown - Bass

Chet Baker - Trumpet

Dizzy Gillespie - Trumpet

Buddy DeFranco - Clarinet

JAZZ ICONS

My own background in jazz goes back to the 1950s, when I was growing up in Great Falls, Montana. Western or "cowboy" music was very popular and it was the music usually played on the radio and jukeboxes. However, there were several Great Falls night clubs, including a black jazz night club called the Ozark Club on the lower south side. During and after WWII, black soldiers stationed at the Great Falls Malstrom Air Force Base could hear jazz and watch other types of entertainment, including tap dancing, comedians, and "exotic" dancers.

There were so few African Americans that I did not know Great Falls was segregated. According to the late Jack Mahood, a white Montana jazz musician who played at the Ozark during the 1940s, there were only two restaurants in the city that served blacks, and one on Central Avenue confined black Ozark musicians to a particular booth and required them to enter through the back door.

Black musicians were not paid as well as white musicians, and I remember that the Ozark piano and drums looked rather shabby. But despite this, the Ozark band of three or sometimes four members was considered so good that prominent white musicians such as the late Harold Nichols would go to the Ozark just to hear them play. Nichols, a white pianist, recalled that national union leaders had forbidden blacks to play with white union bands. The Ozark band was led by the tenor saxophonist the late Bob Mabane, who had played alongside Charlie Parker in 1941 in the Jay McShann orchestra. Mabane was a handsome, gentlemanly figure in the style and manner of Duke Ellington, and it is grotesque to realize he had to go through the back door of a Great Falls restaurant to get a meal or a cup of coffee.

I didn't know Mabane, but he took a personal interest in my high school friend and classmate, the late John Huber, who was teaching himself jazz trumpet. Mabane gave John advice about jazz techniques, and allowed him to sit in occasionally during club performances, even though Huber was underage. My brother Mike, who died in 1961, was a jazz bassist who received informal instruction when he was barely out of grade school from an Ozark musician named "Pops" Teasely. Later, Mike and Huber played jazz together professionally. It was remarkable that these black musicians had so much love for music that they gave special attention to two promising white boys, which was a little risky for everybody, considering the pervasive racism of the time.

Malstrom Air Force Base airmen supported a market for good jazz recordings, and several Great Falls music stores sold high-quality jazz that allowed us to keep up with the innovative jazz of the 1950s, such as be-bop and cool jazz. Huber formed a high school jazz quartet in which he played trumpet, John Nelson played piano, Mike played bass, and I played drums. My drum teacher, the late Ralph Farley, was a white Great Falls jazz musician who taught me jazz drumming techniques, jammed with our quartet, and taught us how to read classical musical scores. Everything considered, we received a lot of good musical instruction we could not get in school at the time. Many people associated jazz with vice, and even today that attitude persists. I recall some Republicans acting as if they had discovered something additionally immoral about President Bill Clinton when they learned he played jazz saxophone.

My drum teacher thought I should study music in college, but I knew my vocation was in the visual arts. I started drawing portraits of jazz musicians in high school, and for many decades continued sketching in jazz nightclubs in the U.S. and Europe. I've always had jazz and classical music playing in the background while I do my artwork, and the rhythm and mood of the music directly affects my hand movements. Later, when I was a professor at the The University of Montana, I was delighted to find that Missoula was a jazz-oriented community. Promoters like Terry Conrad and Joe Korona hosted regular jazz programs on KUFM, and Professor Lance Boyd of the UM Music Department organized jazz work shops for high school and college musicians as part of his annual Buddy DeFranco Jazz Festival. The festival included performances by DeFranco himself, as well as famous jazz musicians from around the world. It was a pleasure for me in mid-life to see that jazz had become a respectable part of academic musical education, and that talented jazz musicians of all races were given the equal respect and admiration they deserved.

The cruel conditions of black slavery and the desire of slaves for their freedom seem to be the roots of this unique American music. The synthesis of sad–blue–and happy emotions in the melody, the syncopated rhythms, and instrumental improvisation are what give jazz its unique quality of freedom and hopeful exuberance. It is no accident that proponents of authoritarian, racist, and totalitarian beliefs have hated jazz. The Nazis called jazz "nigger-Jew" music, the Stalinists called it "degenerate capitalist" music, and the Ku Klux Klan called it "nigger f..." music. Jazz at its best can produce the feeling of liberation in both players and listeners; a feeling that they alone are the masters of their expressive and emotional lives. There is nothing else quite like it.

I recall talking with some friends about Ken Burns' 2001 PBS television documentary *Jazz*, and in general, everyone was pleased with its overall quality, but one of my friends –a jazz musician– was bothered by what he felt was the neglect of important white musicians. I agreed with him because I remembered the 1960s, when a depressing conflict developed about whether whites could play jazz as well as black musicians, and the dispute led to a shameful neglect of the contributions of 1950s West Coast jazz. In hindsight, the argument seems provincial in view of the remarkable understanding, appreciation, and love of jazz shown by people throughout the world; and during the Cold War, jazz may have been one of the U.S.'s most successful weapons in its cultural conflict with Communism. In a 1950s concert in Berlin, the jazz singer Billie Holiday was confronted by a young German musician who begged her to come listen to his jazz band. For two days he followed Billie everywhere, saying, "We swing just like Charlie Parker." Exasperated, she finally agreed to listen to them. Later, she said, "I was never so happy in my life. They were the swingingest cats I ever heard." She remarked that some black people like Parker and herself are born with jazz in their bones, but how impressive it was that people from other countries could play jazz so beautifully just by listening to records.

I knew the dispute about the respective merits of black and white male jazz musicians was a result of the segregation and unequal treatment of black musicians, but neither race has talked much about their own neglect of women in jazz. It wasn't until mid-life that I was conscious of this myself, though now I feel foolish because it seems so obvious. But someone might say, "What about the respect and honors given to Ella Fitzgerald, Billie Holiday, Bessie Smith, etc.?" But the contributions of women were generally limited to vocal jazz, and one only has to peruse the photographs of jazz history to see among the hordes of male musicians the occasional female jazz performer alone like some isolated doe among a herd of water buffalo. Their solitude stimulated the images in my painting "Yellow Skin Girl," and my wood engraving "The Last Dixieland Jazz Band." As hard as it was for any jazz performer–most especially blacks– the difficulties and restrictions for women, particularly black women, were indescribably greater. Women had to be good and self reliant or they didn't stand a chance.

Just as the cultural education of middle-class white women in the first part of the twentieth century was largely restricted to piano, singing, and watercolor painting, black women had similar restrictions. Jazz was just as contaminated by "machismo" culture as any other male-dominated profession, which included my own profession of art. The early blues ballads sung by women are a depressing litany of neglect and abuse, made all the more dispiriting by male indifference. The idea of a woman playing a tuba or trombone was as outlandish as the thought of a lady firing a machine gun. Anita O'Day said that women vocalists were primarily band decorations and were described as the "canaries" of an orchestra. When O'Day demanded and won the right to wear the same orchestra uniform as the male musicians, she was called a lesbian. On the other hand, male musicians could be accused of being too feminine. The saxophone style of Lester Young was sometimes criticized as being soft and unforceful, but the critic Graham Colombe thought that the absence of "machismo" in Lester Young's personality and music was an important reason for the musically sympathetic and close friendship he had with Billie Holiday.

When I first listened to jazz, women vocalists were the occasional intrusion into a world of male instrumentalists, but sometimes they forcefully captured my attention. This first happened in 1954 when I heard Betty Roché's vocal on Duke Ellington's "Take the A Train." Fifty-seven years later, her rendition still gives me the shivers. And when I heard Annie Ross's vocal versions of "Farmer's Market" and "Twisted," it was a surreal and exciting experience to hear a human voice with the hard edged atonal quality of be-bop jazz instruments.

Fortunately, today many of the restrictions on women have disappeared, and it is not unusual to see them playing everything from drums to trumpets. Nonetheless, I decided my catalogue should give the opening lead to early female performers, who–despite male restrictions–made essential contributions to jazz music. My selections are entirely personal and random. I used the same criteria I use for images of male performers. Either the music leads me to the image or an image leads me to the music. It is difficult to find "uncanned" imagery of jazz musicians, and with women performers the need to look celebrated and beautiful is even greater. I do the best with what I come across; sometimes synthesizing my final image from different pictures.

I want to thank Yvonne Seng and the representatives of the Holter Museum for inviting me to show my jazz art at the Museum's 25th Anniversary and to thank all of the contributors who have made this event and catalogue possible. It is gratifying that the festival is educational as well as a musical and artistic event, and it is an honor for me to present my work alongside the performances of professional jazz musicians. It seems fitting that the Poindexter Collection of Abstract Expressionism also is part of the show. Abstract Expressionism–perhaps more than any other visual art form–reflects the type of free, spontaneous improvisation that characterizes jazz music.

James G. Todd, Jr.

I JAZZ PAINTINGS

Scott Joplin
acrylic
24" x 36"
ca 1990-1995

(1868-1917) Born Texarkana, TX
Composer, Piano/Ragtime

Lester Young
acrylic
24" x 36"
ca 1990-1995

(1909-1959) Born Woodville, MS
Tenor Saxophone, Clarinet/Swing

Clifford Brown
acrylic
24" x 36"
ca 1990-1995

(1930-1956) Born Wilmington, DE
Trumpet/Hard Bop

Lennie Tristano
acrylic
24" x 36"
ca 1990-1995

(1919-1978) Born Chicago, IL
Piano, Educator/Cool, Avant-garde

Bix Beiderbecke
acrylic
24" x 36"
ca 1990-1995

(1903-1931) Born Davenport, IA
Cornet/Dixieland

Yellow Skin Girl
acrylic
1985, 36" x 48"

Anonymous

JATP on Tour
acrylic
2005, 36" x 48"

JATP (Jazz at the Philharmonic) from left to right:
Flip Phillips, Ella Fitzgerald, Illinois Jacquet, Lester Young,
Norman Granz, Billie Holiday, Max Roach

Ozark Club Band
acrylic
2010, 24" x 36"

Ozark Club Band (from left to right):
Richard Brown, Bob Mabane, Mike Todd, Chuck Reed

II JAZZ WOMEN

Jazz Women
wood engraving
1994, 12" x 15"

Anonymous

Bessie Smith
wood cut
2012, 16" x 20"

(1894-1937) Born Chattanooga, TN
Vocals/Blues, Classic Jazz

Ella Fitzgerald
wood engraving
1999, 9" x 11"

(1918-1996) Born Newport News, VA
Vocals/Swing, Bop

Anita O'Day
wood cut
2012, 16" x 20"

(1919-2006) Born Chicago, IL
Vocals/Swing, Bop

Billie Holiday
wood cut
2012, 16" x 20"

(1915-1959) Born New York, NY
Vocals/Swing

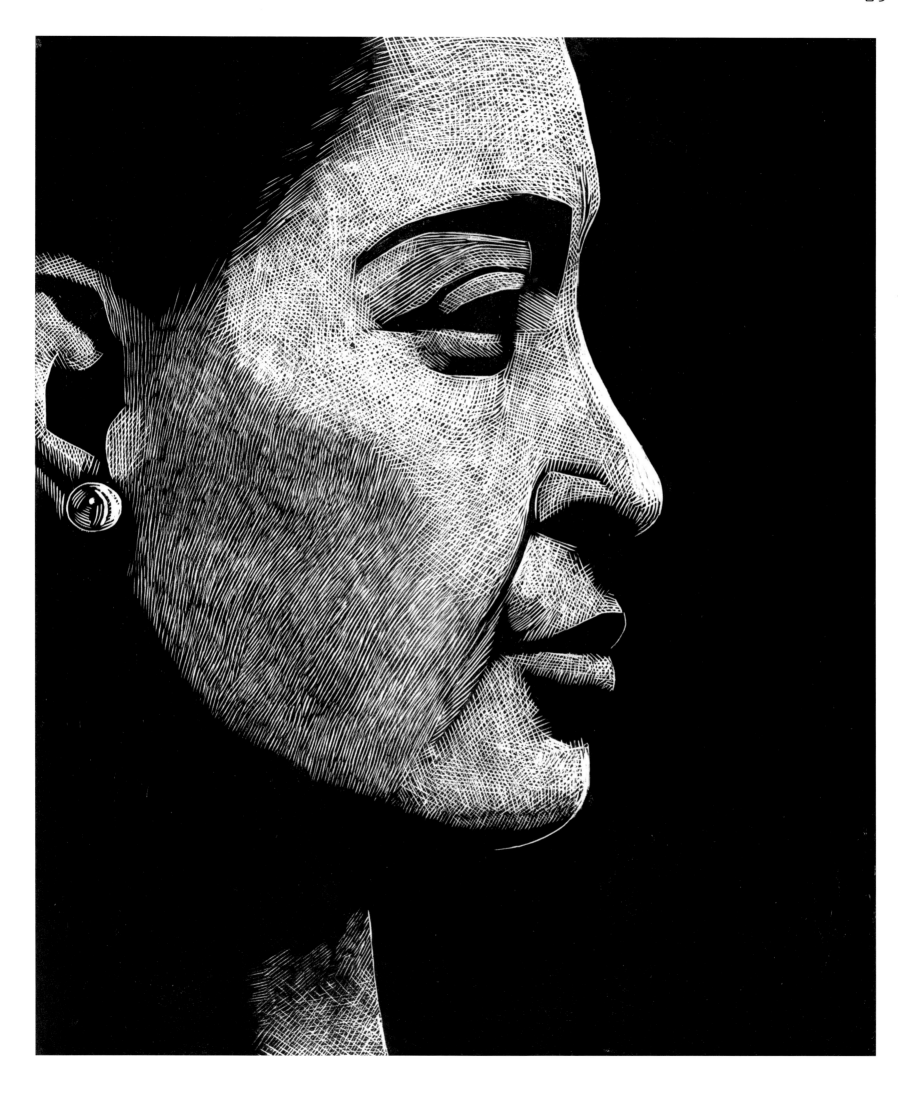

Toshiko Akiyoshi
wood cut
2012, 16" x 20"

(1929-   ) Born Dairen, China
Piano, Arranger, Composer, Leader/Bop, Hard Bop

Lil Hardin Armstrong
wood cut
2012, 12" x 16"

(1901-1971) Born Memphis, TN
Piano, Vocals/Dixieland, Swing

Annie Ross
wood cut
2012, 16" x 20"

(1930-   ) Born Surrey, England
Vocals, Actor/Vocalese, Bop

Betty Roché
wood cut
2012, 12" x 16"

(1920-1999) Born Wilmington, DE
Vocals/Swing

Carla Bley
wood cut
2012, 16" x 20"

(1938-   ) Born Oakland, CA
Piano, Composer, Leader/Post-Bop, Avant-garde

Marian McPartland
wood cut
2012, 16" x 20"

(1920-   ) Born Windsor, England
Piano, Educator/Swing, Bop

Jutta Hipp
wood cut
2012, 9" x 12"

(1925-2003) Born Leipzig, Germany
Piano/Bop, Post-Bop

Shirley Scott
wood cut
2012, 16" x 20"

(1934-2002) Born Philadelphia, PA
Organ, Piano/Hard Bop, Soul Jazz

Beth Lo
wood cut
1995, 24" x 36"

(1949-   ) Born Lafayette, IN
Bass, Vocals/Swing, Rhythm and Blues, Afro-Cuban

Blind Blues Singers
wood cut
1992, 21" x 28"

anonymous

Buddy DeFranco
wood cut
2010, 20" x 16"

(1923-   ) Born Camden, NJ
Clarinet/Bop

Chet Baker
wood engraving
1982, 7" x 8"

(1929-1988) Yale, OK
Trumpet, Vocals/Cool

Charlie Parker
wood engraving
1973, 7" x 9"

(1920-1955) Born Kansas City, KN
Alto Saxophone, Leader, Composer/Bop

Charlie Parker
wood engraving
1973, 7" x 9"

Milt Jackson
wood engraving
1982, 7" x 8"

(1923-1999) Born Detroit, MI
Vibes/Bop, Cool, Hard Bop

Bob Brookmeyer
wood engraving
1990, 7" x 8"

(1929-2011) Born Kansas City, MO
Valve Trombone, Piano, Arranger/Cool, Post-Bop

Chas. Mingus
wood engraving
1982, 7" x 8"

(1922-1979) Born Nogales, AZ
Bass, Piano, Leader, Composer/Bop, Cool, Post-Bop, Avant-garde

Duke Ellington
wood engraving
1982, 7" x 8"

(1899-1974) Born Washington, D.C.
Piano, Composer, Arranger, Leader/Swing, Avant-garde

Gerry Mulligan
wood engraving
1994, 6" x 8"

(1927-1996) Born New York, NY
Baritone Saxophone, Piano, Arranger, Composer, Leader/Cool

Thelonius Monk
wood engraving
1982, 7" x 8"

(1917-1982) Born Rocky Mount, NC
Piano, Composer, Leader/Bop, Post-Bop

Gerry Mulligan with T. Monk
wood engraving
1994, 12" x 14"

Dave Brubeck
wood engraving
2009, 5" x 5"

(1920-   ) Born Concord, CA
Piano, Leader, Composer/Cool, Avant-garde

Abdullah Ibrahim
(Dollar Brand)
wood engraving
2003, 6" x 8"

(1934-   ) Born Capetown, South Africa
Piano, Soprano Saxophone, Cello, Vocals/Bop, Avant-garde, African World Music

David Morgenroth
wood engraving
2010, 10" x 12"

(1961-   ) Born Missoula, MT
Piano/Bop, Post-Bop

Eric Dolphy
wood cut
1966, 8.5" x 11"

(1928-1964) Born Los Angeles, CA
Alto Saxophone, Flute, Bass Clarinet/Cool, Post-Bop, Avant-garde

Lennie Tristano
wood engraving
1995, 11" x 14"

(1919-1978) Born Chicago, IL
Piano, Educator/Cool, Avant-garde

John Huber
wood cut
2012, 16" x 20'

(1938-2009) Born Great Falls, MT
Trumpet, Vibes, Arranger, Leader/Dixieland, Bop

IV JAZZ FANTASIES

Jazz Hustler
wood engraving
1998, 13" x 15"

A synthesis of my interests in jazz and pool playing

Charles Mingus at Paul Desmond's death bed
wood engraving
1995

Chas. Mingus at the bedside of the cancer-ridden
alto saxophonist Paul Desmond (1924-1977)

There is an account that when Desmond was dying of cancer, Charles Mingus came to visit him and found him sleeping. Mingus sat down next to the bed dressed in dark hat and clothes. Desmond related laughingly that when he awoke and saw the figure of Mingus, he thought for a moment that Mingus was the Angel of Death. I imaginatively tried to depict the scene.

The Last Dixieland Jazz Band
wood engraving
2005, 13" x 14"

This picture was done in reaction to the 2005 flooding of New Orleans. I felt that the federal government's incompetent handling of the tragedy reflected its insensitivity to its black citizens and the historical significance of New Orleans as the birth place of jazz.

Jazz Hustlers
wood cut
1990, 36" x 24"

This is a jazz/pool fantasy depicting the machismo nature of traditional North American culture. Hussman's, the Great Falls pool hall where I spent a lot of my youth, with rare exceptions, did not allow women (and I believe blacks) on the premises.

Mike and Jim Todd
wood cut

Image of my brother Mike and me
playing in 1954